REFLECTIONS OF A COTTAGE GARDEN

Deborah R Latchford

Reflections of a Cottage Garden

Vanguard Press

A VANGUARD PAPERBACK

© Copyright 2001
Deborah R Latchford

A CIP catalogue record for this title is
available from the British Library
ISBN 1 903489 06 7

Vanguard Press is an imprint of
Pegasus Elliot MacKenzie Publishers

First Published in 2001

Vanguard Press
Sheraton House Castle Park
Cambridge England

www.pegasuspublishers.com

Printed & Bound in Great Britain

Ivy Studio

"Reflections of a Cottage Garden"
Nature studies, recorded in words
and paintings throughout the year,
including growing tips and specially chosen verses.

Written and illustrated by the author.

Deborah R. Latchford

For Terry, Ruth, Rebecca and Matthew
Mum and Dad

A token of my love

'My Garden of Prayer'
My garden beautifies my yard
and adds fragrance to the air…
But it is also my Cathedral
and my quiet place of prayer…
So little do you realize
that the glory and the power
of He who made the universe
lies hidden in a flower.

INTRODUCTION

This book about my flowers and garden began on: 5th January (my birthday.) A perfect day and year to begin recording my personal thoughts and observations, drawings, painting of birds, insects and flowers found in our cottage garden throughout the four seasons. I plan to complete this work by 31st December. It is hoped you will enjoy my labour of love.

This book is intended as a special keepsake for Terry, Ruth, Rebecca and Matthew. It is my way of sharing my love of nature with you.

I am intrigued with the beauty of flowers, their shapes and growth, nothing seems quite so perfect. Every picture is painted from life, each illustration is life-size and named for identification.

I carefully pick a beautiful bloom each day and put it in a specimen vase and then place it in my studio near the window. I paint the flower and add notes to accompany the painting.

My dad a keen gardener and his father before him, has been an inspiration to me over the years.

I was given my first little garden when I was a young girl. I was always interested in the insects the flowers attracted. I used to collect them in jars and then observe them. I particularly remember the wonderful smell of the freshly dug earth, which has always stayed with me, from those early days.

Now years later…a wife, mum/enthusiastic gardener trained artist with a passionate love of nature.

I can think of no better gift of love to give you!

Lucky flowers for each month:
(An old list which gives the lucky flowers for each month)

January – snowdrop, hope and consolation
February – primrose, young love
March – daffodil, chivalry
April – daisy, innocence
May – lily of the valley, happiness and sweetness
June – rose, love and silence
July – water lilies,
August – gladioli
September – asters
October – dandelion
November – chrysanthemum, cheerfulness under adversity
December – holly, domestic bliss

"Rosemary for Remembrance," the flower stays fresh a long time after being picked.

The pansy means "thinking of you"
The marigold stands for "constancy in love"
The wallflower for "love in the face of adversity"
The lowly thistle means "I will never forget you"
See page 87 Secret language that only flowers can reveal…

January — February

A Saying A Month

January.
The blackest month in all the year
Is the month of Janiveer

February.
Better a wolf in the fold
Than a fine February

Galanthus Nivalis
(Snowdrop)

Primrose
(Primula Vulgaris)

– the 'first roses' –
there are few plants more cheering than the plants'
soft yellow flowers and distinctive rosettes of corrugated
leaves. Although yellow is the most familiar colour, primroses
also come in shades of red, purple, pink and white, appeared much earlier this year!
double primroses see

Growing tips
Plant from Autumn to Spring 12in apart, in ordinary garden soil,
in sun or light shade.
Sow seeds in late spring or summer in a cold frame or divide after flowering

8th January

I have decided this will be the day to start painting the first flowers of the month and write this page.

Jasminum Nudiflorum

Our winter flowing Jasmine (Jasminum Nudiflorum) is so cheerful in the garden at this time of year. It has been in bloom since last November and will continue to flower until March. Glorious sprays of golden starry flowers on bare twigs, reaches a height of 10 ft. I named our cottage after this shrub, growing beside the porch. It is trained loosely against the wall, the branches tumble down. This plant was first introduced to this country in 1844 and brought here from China. It is not strictly a climber but a shrub.

Although a frost will spoil the open blooms, it does not affect the bronze-tinted buds lined up waiting to replace them.

Growing tips:

The flower is best trained on trellis against any but an eastern facing wall or fence. Prune in spring by cutting the flowered shoots back to near their base, taking out weak and old stems at ground level and tying in replacement shoots.

Viola

Garden pansies (Viola) are among the best loved of all garden plants. I must confess they are my favourites. The winter flowering pansies start to bloom in autumn and in a mild winter such as this, will continue to flower until late spring.

Given a lightly shaded position and a moist soil, each plant quickly forms a well spread tuft of colour 6-9" high and 12" across. I dead head regularly or the plants seed themselves to death. Pansies provide splashes of colour throughout the year.

Growing tips:

Pansies and Violas give of their best when raised as biennials, though they will flower the same year from seeds sown under glass in spring. For winter, spring and summer flowering biennials, sow in an outdoor nursery bed during summer, thin seedlings to 4" and transport to flowering sites in autumn, 10" apart.

Jasmine Nudiflorum

Winter flowering pansy - Viola
(Universal Mixed f1)

Hedera C 'Dentata Variegata' (Persian Ivy)

A beautiful Ivy, it covers the back wall of the cottage. Each leaf has a central green area that merges, through grey-green, into a broad pale yellow edge. It is a truly eye-catching climber, left to its own devices on a wall, the plant can swarm to a height of 20-30ft. I have to trim around the windows, the great luxuriant leaves sometimes reach a length of 12", the leaves certainly vary in size, and the leaves I chose to paint are the smallest.

Growing tips:

Plant between autumn and spring, in any good, well-drained soil. A sunny position produces better-coloured variegation. Prune in spring and/or summer by thinning out old and woody stems and by reducing long new shoots.

Cotoneaster Horizontalis

We have two planted against a wall and one against a fence. In shape and texture, in its seasonal changes in foliage and from flower to fruit, cotoneaster is quite beautiful. On flat ground it seldom grows more than 2ft. high, but planted against walls its fans of tiny leaves will climb much higher. The branches cascade outwards and downwards. In May tiny white and pink flowers appear, queen wasps find these irresistible. Bright red berries are accompanied in late autumn by equally brilliant leaves.

Growing tips:

Plant between autumn and spring in ordinary well-drained soil and in full sun. Prune lightly, if at all, in late spring.

Berginia Cordifolia

Known to me as elephant ears, large, thick paddle shaped leaves are, unlike the foliage of most herbaceous plants, truly every green. Valuable for ground cover, slow spreading. The thick flowers stems have almost reached full height of about 12" with sprays of pale pink, bell shaped blooms. Quite lovely! Dad gave me this wonderful plant!

Growing tips:

Plant between autumn and spring, in ordinary soil, in light shade or sun 12" apart. Remove faded flower stems, leave plants undisturbed until crowding encourages division in autumn or spring.

Privet (Ligustrum Vulgare)

In July, this privet flowers, similar to white lilac, followed by lovely black berries in autumn.

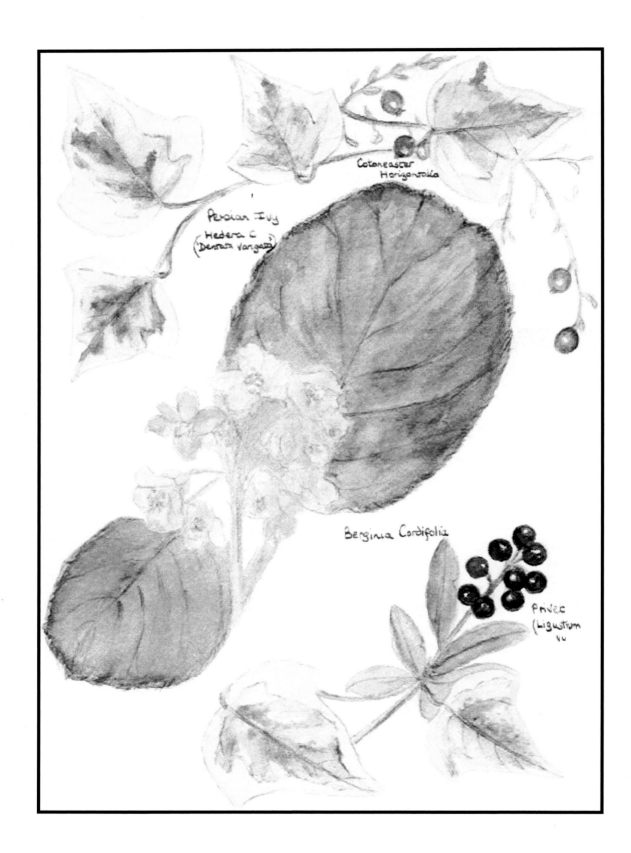

Cotoneaster
Horizontalis

Persian Ivy
Hedera C
('Dentata Variegata)

Berginia Cordifolia

Privet
(Ligustrum
vu

Spring has arrived!

Forsythia 'Suspensa'

Long streamers of large lemon yellow flowers on arching, interlacing branches, bright and cheerful, fully hardy – 10ft. high and wide. We have three bushes, they are years old, and every year they give their best in colour and bloom.

Growing tips:

Plant between autumn and spring, in ordinary soil and in sun or light shade. Propagate by hardwood cuttings in autumn, flowers are born on wood from the previous year. Prune after flowering, shortening young shoots by one-third. Then remove a few old shoots from ground level annually.

Chaenomeles Speciosa (Japanese Quince)

The quince makes a twiggy bush 6ft. or more tall, with a spread of 5-7ft. Sometimes a flower or two opens in mid-winter, just buds at present, and has brilliant scarlet flowers. It is well in bloom by March.

Growing tips:

Plant between autumn and spring in any type of moisture-retentive soil, if possible in full sun. Propagate by cutting in late summer, or by layering in autumn. Prune to maintain shape after flowering.

Crocus Aureus 'Dutch Yellow'

Cheerful sights in the garden, they look best grouped together. If the crocus are planted in grass, this must not be cut until the plant leaves have withered in late spring. I prefer the crocus in the border beneath deciduous shrubs. We have a good show each year, they brighten our days.

Growing tips:

Plant winter and spring flowering crocuses as soon as available in autumn. Set the crocus 2.3" deep and 4" apart, multiply in number each year.

Myosotis Sylvatica (Forget-me-not)

Delightful tiny pure blue flowers, each with a white or yellow eye.

Growing tips:

Seeds freely, dad gave me my first plant, now the garden is full.

Galanthus Nivalus (Snowdrop)

'Fair Maids of February' the common wild species together with its double flowered form look best in drifts beneath deciduous trees.

Growing tips:

Plant in September 2/3" deep and apart, once established they seed themselves.

Primula Polyanthus

A popular plant since its introduction in the 19th century. It's 9-12" high flower size decreases after the first year, plants become leafier, and then divide after flowering.

Forsythia
'Suspensa'

Chaenomeles
Speciosa
(Japanese Quince)

Myosotis
Sylvatica
(forget-me-not)

'Dutch yellow'
Crocus

Galanthus nivalis
(Snow drop)

Primula
'Barnhaven' Polyanthus

We have had severe winds, apparently more to come – started in January and it's late February now!

Common Ivy (Hedera Helix)

It's verdure trails
the Ivy shoot
Along the ground
from root to root...

I am fond of Ivy, I love it's clinging habit, Rebecca suggested I name the studio – Ivy Studio.

Kerria Japonica (Jew's Mallow) 'Pleniflora'

It is known also as bachelor's buttons. Introduced from China in 1804, a lovely elegant arching shrub, slender green stems, hidden by shaggy, butter-yellow double blooms 2" across, has a height and spread of 4-6ft. Terry's mum gave me this plant.

Growing tips:

Plant from autumn to spring, in any soil, in sun or shade. Propagate from rooted suckers or cuttings in autumn, and if necessary prune hard after flowering and remove annually some older stems.

Vinca Minor (Lesser Periwinkle)

A lovely evergreen plant, spreads quickly, with pretty blue-mauve flowers.

Growing tips:

Plant from autumn to spring, in ordinary well drained, deep and moist soil, and in the shade. Excellent ground cover if spaced 12-18" apart. Propagate by division during dormancy.

Hyacinth Orientalis (Dutch Hyacinth)

Deliciously scented spikes of starry soft blue-mauve flowers, and they look delightful grouped together.

Growing tips:

Plant in autumn 4-6" deep and 10-12" apart, and dead head after flowering.

Pulmonaria Saccharata (Lungwort)

Most attractive plants, known as Ladies and Gentleman. Lungwort is derived from the latin 'pulmo' meaning 'lung' probably because the spotted leaves resembled the lungs. Useful as ground cover, the long, hairy oval leaves are green splashed with silver, heads of flowers appear at the top of 12 in stems. They begin as pink, then mauve to blue, the foliage develops fully only after the flowers have faded.

Growing tips:

Plant from early autumn to early spring 10" apart in moist soil and in semi-shade. Propagate by division in autumn or spring.

Primula Vulgaris (Primrose)

Primroses remain a firm favourite of mine, attractive and a welcome splash of extra colour in spring.

Growing tips: See page 12

Viola Labrodoric 'Purpurea' (Violet)

This delightful sweet smelling violet is so pretty and an old-fashioned favourite of mine. A wanderer by nature, self-propagating, forms attractive low ground cover of rich lilac-mauve flowers. Ruth's birthday flower!

Growing tips:

The plant does best in the shade.

Common Ivy
(Hedera Helix)

Kerria Japonica
(Jew's Mallow)

Vinca
Mino
(Lesser periwin

Hyacinth orientalis
(Dutch Hyacinth)

Pulmonaria
Saccharata (Lungwort)

Primula
Vulgaris
(Primrose)

Viola labradorica
'Purpurea' (VIOLET)

25

March 1st St. David's Day

The land returns from winter
Like the Saint from pilgrimage
Bringing with him a bird and a flower
Over mountains like dragons turned to stone.

Today repeats the yearly miracle
Along the valleys of the daffodil
And in the brightening sky above
St. David's emblem is the dove

Mothering Sunday

In the time before Bank Holiday's
Farmer's boys and servant girls
Left the farm or big houses early
Going home for the day
On Mothering Sunday
Though home was miles away
With flowers for their mother's present
Gathered as they went.

It's different these days
All you have to do is stop
At the flower shop
With the pocket money you've saved
And the daffodils there
Came by train or even by plane;
But the present still means the same
For the language of flowers doesn't change

March — April

March
March comes in like a lion
And goes out like a lamb

April
April showers
bring summer flowers.

Daisy
(Bellis perennis)
Favourite garden plants, have been cultivated for centuries
They bear a profusion of flowers from April to July. Growing tips Sow in early summer
transplanting to flowering site
in Autumn. 8in apart
Dead-head to prevent early
seeding

Daffodil
(Narcissus pseudo-narcissus)
This yellow trumpet daffodil brings cheer on the dullest of days,
because its flowers never close up, no matter how bad the weather
15in high, is best grown in drifts. In March and April it
sings the praises of early spring from almost any position.

Growing tips
Plant the bulbs 6in apart. Propagate all narcissi by lifting them
as the leaves die down and removing the smaller bulbs round the parent

27

Easter

This is the end of winters reign
When the squirrel had to hide
When the swallows fled to the south
All the summer flowers died

When the snows took over the mountain tops
When the frost had the fields in an iron hold
When the ice shut the swans out of the ponds
And the world was imprisoned by cold

Winter has passed! The birds return
The seeds beneath the stone has found
A way to the light and like a knife
The daffodil prizes open the ground

Buds and bulbs break out of their bonds
And squirrels were only sleeping and survive
By the yearly miracle
That keeps the world alive

Narcissus triandus 'Thalia.'

The species Narcissus triandus comes from the mountains of Northern Spain. 'Thalia' is taller and more robust than the species – 10-15" high, has larger flowers with creamy-white blooms in April.

Growing tips:

Plant 6in. apart, quite beautiful!

Tulip, Darwin Group

Darwin tulips are notable for their rich colours, 'Scarlett O'Hara' is 2ft. tall. My favourite – most cheerful.

Growing tips:

Plant 6-8" apart.

Narcissus Pseudonarcissus 'Golden Harvest' (wild daffodil, Lent Lily)

See page March-April.

Growing tips:

Best grown in drifts in long grass beneath trees or, as Wordsworth noted: 'beside the water.'

Leucojum aestivum (summer snowflakes)

2ft. tall, near relatives of snowdrops.

Growing tips:

Plant in late summer or early autumn, 4" deep 6-8" apart in moist soil.

Muscari armen Lacum (grape hyacinth)

8" high, a common grape hyacinth spreads extensively. In April it bears densely packed rich blue flowers with white rims, tends to stay in clumps.

Growing tips:

Plant in late summer or early autumn, 3" deep and apart.

Cheiranthus Chieri (wallflower)

Neat 15-18" high plants, bloom from April/May-July, sometimes put on early display in autumn when they are planted out.

Growing tips:

Sow outdoors in early summer and transplant in autumn 12" apart. After transplanting to flowering sites, pinch out the growing tips to encourage branching.

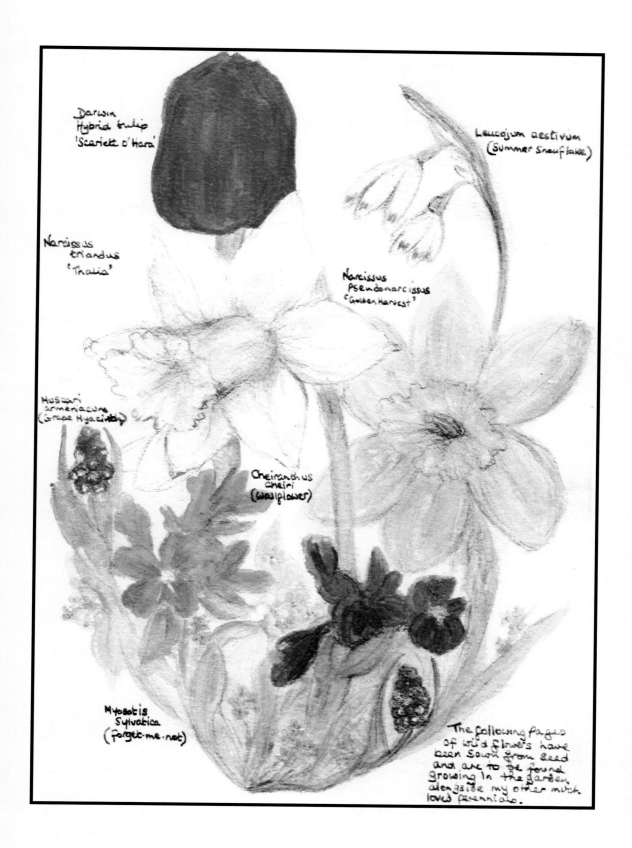

Darwin
Hybrid tulip
'Scarlett o'Hara'

Leucojum aestivum
(Summer Snowflake)

Narcissus
triandus
'Thalia'

Narcissus
Pseudonarcissus
'Golden Harvest'

Muscari
armeniacum
(Grape Hyacinth)

Cheiranthus
cheiri
(Wallflower)

Myosotis
Sylvatica
(Forget-me-not)

The following pages
of wild flowers have
been sown from seed
and are to be found
growing in the garden,
alongside my other much
loved perennials.

31

Wild Flower Gardening 'Seeds'

Wildflowers require as much care and understanding as their more robust garden relatives.

Ox-eye Daisy or Moon Daisy

The large Ox-eye Daisy, which should be seen on a moonlit evening to appreciate its alternative name of Moon Daisy as it appears like small shining moons among the grass **Marsh Marigold**, its unopened flower buds preserved in vinegar were used to replace the true Mediterranean casper.

Cornflower or Bluebottle

The cornflower was once the companion of all field plants, especially corn. It was probably a native of the Mediterranean and the orient, and became widespread in prehistoric Europe, later spreading to other parts of the world. The flowers contain a beautiful blue dye based upon the pigment cyanin. This is soluble in water, and is used to colour perfumes, wool, aromatic spices and even champagne wines.

Everyone should find a place for
wildflowers in their garden. They
possess a simple beauty so often
lacking in bold, brash bedding plants,
and have the bonus of playing an
essential part in
encouraging wildlife, and
feeding bees and butterflies.

Cornflower
Centaurea Cyanus

Field Poppy
Papaver
rhoe

Ox-eye Daisy
Chrysanthemum
Leucanthemum

Sun Spurge
Euphorbia helioscopia

Lady's Smock
Cardamine Pratensis

Marsh Marigold
Caltha Palustris

Self-heal
Prunella Vulgaris

Cowslip
Primula Veris

orange-tip
butterfly

Wood Anemone
Anemone nemorosa

Ground Ivy
Glechoma hederacea

Silverweed
Potentilla anserina

Field poppy

The field poppy is one of the most attractive weeds. The field poppy contains, especially in its flowers, poisonous alkaloids, which can be harmful to people and animals. Its petals were used in the past as a cough medicine. They were also used as a substitute for tea.

Sun Spurge

The sun spurge contains a poisonous white, milky juice, which causes inflammation of the digestive tract in domestic animals. It can also cause severe irritation, and even blindness, if it comes into contact with the eyes.

Lady's Smock or Cuckoo Flower

The Cuckoo flower is one of the food plants of the lovely orange-tipped butterfly. The flowers are rich in nectar, and the content of vitamin C in the leaves is very substantial, being five times higher than in lemons.

Cowslip

It grew particularly well in the close vicinity of cowpats, called then cowslips or flops, and so the name was coined.

Wood Anemone

It will grow in any but the most acid or waterlogged ground, its natural habitat is deciduous woodland.

Self-Heal

It had a great reputation as a wound herb and cure for sore throats, a flower of dry grassland.

Silverweed

The flowering stems were formerly used in the treatment of stomach and intestinal disorders, and for bathing wounds slow to heal.

Ground Ivy

In olden days the ground ivy was used to cure diseases of the breathing tract, to get rid of coughs, and for bathing ulcerous wounds.

Stinking Iris (affectionately know to me as Pam's uncle Wilfred's Iris)

This delightful Iris with its attractive berries was given to me by my good friend and neighbour Pam. The Stinking Iris is so called because the leaves, when crushed, give off a sweet sickly smell, which some think is like meat and accounts for an alternative name of the Roast Beef Plant. The berries in their open capsules last a long time.

Evening Primrose

Such a beautiful plant. The seeds can remain dormant for at least 40 years.

Common Mullein

Very tall and robust. The plant is adapted to dry conditions, as it is densely clothed in whitish hairs, which protect it from excessive dehydration and overheating.

Dame's Violet

Cultivated for many centuries as a garden plant, with medium to tall erect, biennial or perennial large white or purple flowers, which are sweetly scented.

Welsh poppy

The Welsh Poppy loves damp, rocky places. It stands 12" high with fresh green leaves. It has soft yellow or orange flowers, single or double that bloom throughout summer.

Nettle-leaved Bellflower

When in flower in midsummer like all other bellflowers it lasts well into September. It is a tall perennial. (Pam gave this plant to me.)

Goatsbeard

Goatsbeard has earned another name of: Jack-go-to-bed-at-noon. At mid-day the flower closes up. Before the beautiful, completed spherical seed head develops, the pappus (the ring of feathery hairs surrounding the seed, enabling it to be carried on the wind) forms a beard. In the middle ages the taproot was eaten as a carrot.

Red Campion

Red Campion has teeth, which are tightly rolled back. The flowers are bright rose pink.

Jacob's Ladder

Jacob's Ladder is a medium to tall perennial forming tufts with erect angled stems, and the flowers are blue, and occasionally white.

Corn Marigold

Corn Marigold so pestilent a weed was the brilliant yellow Corn Marigold to farmers that King Henry 11 decreed it should be destroyed whenever it appeared, probably the first flower to receive the royal death warrant. It can still be found on disturbed ground.

Green Alkanet

Green Alkanet is a flower of the hedgerow, which has naturalized in Southwest Britain, having been introduced in the Middle Ages as a dye plant.

Common Mouse-ear

The Common Mouse ear has sepals the same length as the petals and flowers from April to November.

Lesser Celadine

Lesser Celadine, it dies away completely in May, when it has finished flowering.

Birdsfoot Trefoil

Birdsfoot Trefoil is one of the most common members of the pea family,

Creeping Jenny

Creeping Jenny, it was a wound herb, and used against 'all issues of blood in man or woman.'

Herb Bennet

Herb Bennet is a medium, hairy perennial with stems erect from May to September.

Slender St. Johns Wort

Slender St. Johns Wort is one of the smallest of the family.

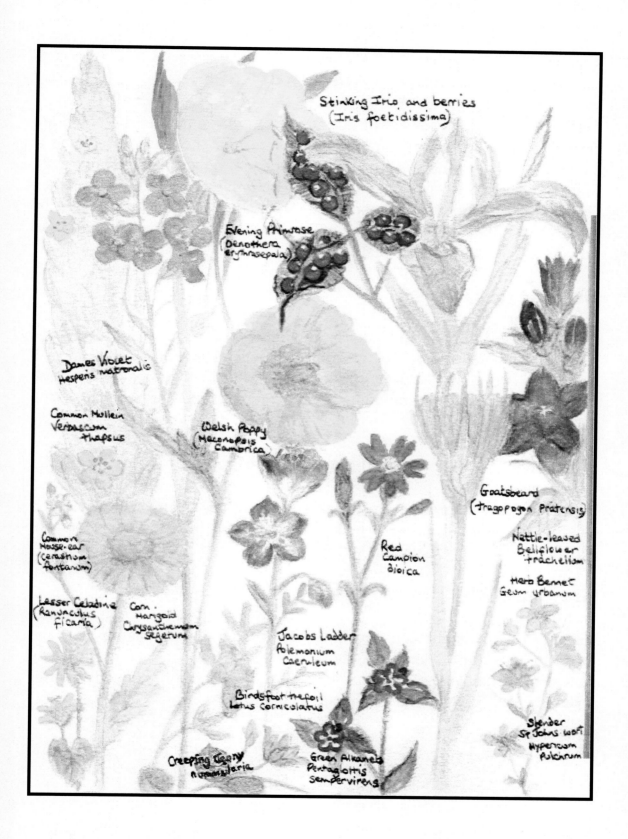

Stinking Iris and berries
(Iris foetidissima)

Evening Primrose
(Oenothera
erythrosepala)

Dames Violet
Hesperis matronalis

Common Mullein
Verbascum
thapsus

Welsh Poppy
(Meconopsis
Cambrica)

Goatsbeard
(Tragopogon pratensis)

Common
House-ear
(Cerastium
fontanum)

Red
Campion
dioica

Nettle-leaved
Bellflower
trachelium

Herb Bennet
Geum urbanum

Lesser Celandine
(Ranunculus
ficaria)

Corn.
Marigold
Chrysanthemum
segetum

Jacobs Ladder
Polemonium
Caeruleum

Birdsfoot trefoil
Lotus corniculatus

Slender
St Johns wort
Hypericum
pulcnrum

Creeping Cizary
nummularia

Green Alkanet
Pentaglottis
sempervirens.

Clematis Montana 'Rubens'

The pretty rose pink flowers of our 5-year-old clematis over the porch are carried in May in such quantities as almost to hide the leaves. But such is its vgour – it can climb to 40ft. – that it tends to produce a tangle of growth. The best course is to encourage it up a tree, climbing rose or pergola. When the main shoots reach a horizontal support some way up, they should be trained carefully along it, and they will than let fall a cascade of foliage and flowers, a superb show this year!

Growing tips:

Plant between autumn and late spring, they resent root disturbance and should be planted out as pot grown specimens. They should be put in a position where stems and flowers are in the sun but the roots are cool, moist and shaded. They should be pruned immediately after their flowering period in late spring or early summer.

Camelia C. Sinensis

This beautiful evergreen from China and Japan has lustrous foliage and a single cup shaped flowers of pink. Invaluable for bringing beauty to our garden in late winter and early spring.

Growing tips:

Generally hardy in Britain, are lime haters, will tolerate neutral soil and thrive in light to deep shade. A site near a west, south or even north facing wall is quite suitable. Propagate by leaf bud or semi-hardwood cuttings under glass in summer and then dead head after flowering.

Primula Polyanthus or bunch-flowered primrose

These large flowered cheerful hybrids produce blooms in compact long clusters on tall sturdy stems 9-12" high. The flowers appear from March to early May. The flower size decreases after the first year and the plants become leafier. I usually divide after flowering.

Growing tips:

Can be grown from seed in a cold greenhouse or frame from spring until midsummer for planting out in autumn. They need a fertile moist soil and do best in light shade.

Clematis
montana
'Rubens'

April
The roofs are shining from the rain.
the sparrows twitter as they fly
And with a windy April grace
The little clouds go by

Yet the back yards are bare and brown
With only one unchanging tree –
I could not be so sure of Spring
Save that it sings to me.

Camelia
C. Salvenensis

Primula
Polyanthus

Myosotis
Sylvatica (forget me not)

Syringa Vulgaris 'Madame Lemoine' Lilac

The flowering season is short, but the hardy fragrance of the flower heads is as irresistible as the sight of them tossing lightly in the breeze above a sea of heart-shaped leaves 12ft. high and almost as wide in May-June. A welcome sight by our front gate.

Growing tips:

Propagation is easier by heel cuttings in late summer, or by layering. Pruning of all syringas consist of dead-heading after flowering and then in early autumn remove weak and crossing branches.

Rosa 'Canary Bird'

One of the earliest roses to appear, beautiful yellow flowers in May and June. Both its parents, Rosa Xanthina and Rosa Hugonis, are lovely plants too. So it starts from a good genetic base. I have this growing with a passion flower trained over the window in our front garden.

Growing tips:

Plant species roses in the same manner as Hybrid teas; they require little pruning apart from the removal of soft tips and straggly grows. Propagate by cuttings or by seeds obtained from the hips and sown when ripe, in a cold frame.

Lunaria Annua (Honesty)

Although this Honesty (also known as Lunaria Biennis) can well be grown as an annual, it is naturally a biennial. Flowers April to June are pale lavender in the species and range from rich purple and red in garden forms. Lunaria 'Alba' has pure white flowers and are succeeded in summer by fruits that split to reveal almost transparent, disc-shaped membranes, which can be dried and used for winter flower arrangements. It is these round silvery cases that lead to its Latin name Lunaria, derived from luna meaning 'moon' and also provided one of its common names, moonwort.

Growing tips:

Sow in outdoor nursery beds in summer, thin seedlings to 6" apart, and transplant to the flowering site in early autumn, 12in. apart, self sows freely.

Fritillaria Meleagris (Snakes Head)

Large drooping bells whose squared markings are in deep purple, tall stems and the few narrow grey-green leaves give the whole plant a graceful appearance.

Growing tips:

Plant in late summer or autumn, 4" deep and 6" apart.

Pulsatilla Vulgaris (Pasque Flower)

The Pasque flower, as its name implies, is a flower of Easter.

Growing tips:

Plant in autumn, 8-10" apart in well drained soil.

Endymion Hispanicus (Spanish Bluebell)

They are fine robust plants on 12" spikes, they flower April to June. There are a number of attractive named hybrid forms, pure white and in shades of blue and pink.

Growing tips:

Plant bulbs in autumn 4-6" deep.

Primula Vulgaris see Jan-Feb.

Syringa Vulgaris
"Madame Lemoine"
(Lilac)

Rosa
"Canary Bird"

Lunaria annua
(Honesty, Moonwort,
Moneywort)

'Alba'

Endymion
hispanicus
(Spanish bluebell)

Fritillaria
Maleagris
(Snakes Head)

Primula

Pulsatilla Vulgaris
(Pasque Flower)
red

CUCKOO

Cuckoo, cuckoo what do you do
In April, I open my bill
In May, I sing night and day
In June, I change my tune
In July, up high I fly
In August, away I must.

May — June

Lily of the Valley.
It has an unforgettable perfume
The bell-like flowers always nod
to one side of the main flower stalk
Legend has it that they represent
the tears of the Virgin Mary shed
at the foot of the Cross

Growing tips
Grow in a shady site fairly dry woodland
Propagate by division of the rhizomes
in Autumn

Lily of the Valley
Convallaria majalis

May
Who shears his sheep before St Servatuss Day
Loses his wool more than his sheep.

June
A cold and wet June spoils the rest of the year

Dog Roses (Rosa Canina)

Roses are among the flowers longest favoured by man. The Ancient Greeks and Romans used the petals for perfume and even for carpeting. In the theory of signatures the thorn is said to resemble a dog's tooth, and according to Pliny, a Roman soldier bitten by a mad dog applied the roots of the rose to the wound to cure it, hence the Dog Rose.

After the Rain

I wonder, when the rain is past,
And I'm allowed outside at last,
Why all the garden seems to look
like pictures in a picture book

The colours all look flat and light
Like paint-box colours, shiny – bright,
With every flower-face washed quite clean,
And every leaf a greener green

While all the boughs are black as ink
In fact it looks, I really think
As if God took his paint-box out
to paint the colours all about

For all the blues are bluer yet
And see! His paint is still quite wet!
Oh yes indeed, I'm sure it looks
Like children's coloured picture books.

Rose- "My love"
Meaning love and silence
(Matthews birthday flower)

25th May

For Jerry
The day of your operation
~ triple by pass ~
I picked this rose to express my love
for you, this verse I dedicate to you

My Dearest Husband

Someone who means to me
more than my life,
Someone whose love is a shelter
from strife,
Someone whom I can start everyday,
feeling better and wiser for going his way

Someone who stands like a bulwark
from fears,
Someone whose love is indefinitely dear,
Someone who never has failed me,
although things have been uphill with
rough ties to go

Someone who closes the door on defeat,
Someone who makes life unbelievably sweet,
Someone who understands all that I feel,
Someone who makes life's high song
become real

Someone who'd love me until my life ends,
Someone who's closer even than friends,
Someone whose loyalty burns like a flame.
Someone who gave me his heart ♥
and his name.

Deborah
Your everloving wife X

The Rose
Love it is a flower and you its only seed
Just remember in the winter far beneath the bitter snow
lies the seed that with the sun's love, in the spring, becomes the rose.

50

Lonicera Periclymenum (Honeysuckle 'Serotina')

This plant has been a cottage garden favourite for centuries. 'Serotina' the late Dutch Honeysuckle flowers in late May or June with its heads of pale yellow, purple-red blooms sends out heady waves of fragrance, it grows to 15-20 ft. and climbs over the porch to accompany the clematis Montana and passiflora caerulea, all vigorous climbers

Growing tips:

Plant in the spring, and in any kind of well manured, well drained soil. Propagate by cutting in summer or autumn, by layering or by seeds. The common Honeysuckle is prone to aphid attacks, so spray with malathion before infestation becomes severe.

Aguilegia Columbine

Latin word Columba for doves. The flower was said to resemble a group of five doves.

Rhododendron Ponticum

Vigorous evergreen shrub, flowers are mauve, lovely shiny leaves. We have two well- established shrubs; it flowers in June, and can grow up to 60ft. high. It is well to remember that many Rhododendron are woodland plants, and that though they accept (with sufficient moisture) the sun, their growth habit is more delicate in half shade.

Growing tips:

Plant in autumn or spring, they thrive in moist, acid soil. After flowering, dead head unless seeds are wanted, and remove the flowers by hand.

Ceanothus 'Delight' (Californian Lilac)

A native of California, where they are known as blue blossom, or California lilacs. Glossy foliage and an abundance of small blue to purple-blue flowers in late spring. Although hardy, it still benefits from a warm south or west-facing wall. We have three well- established shrubs and can grow to 10ft.

Growing tips:

Plant in late spring, in good well drained, preferably neutral soil. It is best in full sun and, ideally should be grown against a sheltered wall. Propagate by cuttings in summer and prune after flowering, shortening young shoots to 3".

Veronica Longifolia (Ladies Needlework)

Robust, medium to tall perennial. Its flowers are lilac or pale-blue, on tall erect stems and slender pointed flower spikes in June-July. My dad gave this plant to me, a good show each year.

Growing tips:

Grow from seed or plant division.

Lupinus Polyphylius

Another of the indispensables for a herbaceous border. It was first introduced to Britain in 1826.

Growing tips:

Grow from seed.

Lathyrus Latifolius

Graceful and their foliage is attractive, and grows to 10ft. (It looks good when trained along the fence in our front garden.)

Growing tips:

Grow from seed.

Anemone Colonaria 'De Caen'

The wild species of which this anemone is a strain grows on the Mediterranean hillside, and grows less than 12" high with 1½ to 2" wide flowers in pure vivid hues.

Growing tips:

Soak the rhizomes for several hours before planting 1½ to 2" deep, 4" apart.

Lonicera
Honeysuckle
'Serotina'

Rhododendron
Ponticum

Aquilegia
glandulosa
Columbine

Lupinus
Polyphyllus

Ceanothus
'Delight'

Veronica
longifolia
(ladies
needlework)

Anemone
Colonaria
'De Caen'

Lathyrus latifolius
(everlasting sweet pea)
(Rebecca's birthday flower)

54

Whether the Weather be fine

Whether the weather be fine
or whether the weather be not
whether the weather be cold
or whether the weather be hot
We'll weather the weather
Whatever the weather
whether we like it or not.

Scarlet pimpernai
Angallis arvensis

WEATHER WISE
FORECASTING FROM FLOWERS

Common plants and flowers, which react to changes in the weather:

PLANT	REACTION
Burnet Saxifrage	Half-open flowers mean weather clearing
Chickweed	Half-open flowers mean weather clearing
Clover	Contracts leaves before a storm
Convolvalus	Closes petals before rain
Daisy	Closes petals before rain
Dandelion	Closes petals before rain
Gentian	Folds leaves and closes flowers before rain
Lime	Leaves cover flowers before rain
Ox-eye Daisy	Closes flowers before rain
Purple Sandwort	Closes petals before rain
Rock Rose	Flowers droop before rain
Sow Thistle	Flowers open before rain, and close in sun
Speedwell	Closes petals before rain

Trefoil	Stem swells before rain
Tulip	Closes petals before rain
Wood Anemone	Flowers close and droop before rain.

Scarlet Pimpernell is known in some country areas as:

The Ploughman's weather glass.

On fine mornings it will be found with its flowers widely extended, but once humidity reaches a critical figure, probably around 80% it closes up the petals to protect the pollen.

WHAT THE BIRDS AND BEES FORETELL

Fish bite the least
When the wind is in the east

It's a sure sign of rain when cats wash behind their ears

If bees stay at home, rain will soon come
If bees fly away, fine will be the day.

When dogs eat grass
Fine days soon past

Swallows high, staying dry,
Swallows low, wet twill blow

Cockerel before two in the morning
Of two days wet it is a warning

SIMPLE OBJECTS THAT CAN REGISTER WEATHER CHANGES

Pine cones

These fruits of the pine open their needles before fine weather and closes them before the rain.

Landmarks

Hills, Church steeples or other distant objects seem to be 100 metres closer and clearer before rain.

Sounds

Noises made by distant traffic, planes or birdcalls seem nearer before the rain.

Smoke

Descending smoke is usually a sign of rain.

Milk and cream

These will often go sour if left standing outside a refrigerator when a storm is near.

Seaweed

A piece of seaweed hung up in a shed or outhouse reacts to changes in atmosphere humidity, and when it feels damp-wet weather on the way.

Dust

Small eddies of swirling dust near the ground on a hot, fine day – less settled conditions to aching corns, and rheumatic twinges – rain on the way.

Garden Visitors

Wren

our regular visitor,
to my delight, nested
the Ivy this year

Blue tit

Blackbird

Dawn

The thrush is tapping a stone
With a snail's shell in its beak.
A small bird hangs from a cherry
Until the stem shall break.

No waking song has begun
And yet birds chatter and hurry
And throng in the elms gloom
Because an owl goes home.

Song thrush

Patience

As the soil, makes the young plants grow
and as seeds unfold in a garden,
so will God make goodness and Songs of Praise
spring up in all the world.

The Cottage Garden

The summer air is fragrant with a delicate bouquet
of lavender and candytuft and pungent mint and bay
The heady scent of roses as they slumber in the heat
The tang of golden marigolds and honeysuckle sweet
The simply cottage garden in its perfumed disarray
enchants our keenest senses in a most delightful way

My favourite annuals –

Clarkia

Godetia

Seeds
Purchased from:–
Thompson & Morgan
A useful garden tip,
passed on to me by
my dear friend Mr King
Mix the seeds in damp
sand, helps germination

Lavatera
'Silver Cup'

Cosmos

Lavatera
'Mont blanc'

Candytuft
Dwarf fairy Mixed
"mini
Mopcaps"

Bearded Iris

The brilliant exquisitely scented flowers are carried like medieval banners, on strong stems above the spears of foliage; my friend Pat gave this Iris to me from her Mum's garden. I love it! Although it is in flower for a short time, it is a magnificent specimen.

Growing Tips:

Plant between midsummer and early autumn, setting the top of the rhizomes level with the soil surface and spacing 12" apart, tall types 18" apart. Propagate by division of the rhizomes – replanting only the younger, outer sections immediately after flowering, and preferably every three years in order to maintain flowering vigour.

Paeonia Officinalis (Apothecaries Peony)

The wild single-flowered species were brought here from Southern Europe in the 16th century, and within 100 years double forms were in cultivation. The plant became know as the 'Apothecaries Peony' and as late, as the beginning of this century, in Sussex children wore peony-root necklaces to ward off toothache.

Growing Tips:

Plant between autumn and spring, 3-4 ft. apart. Most peonies take a couple of years to settle, but once established they will flourish in the same site for up to 50 years. Propagation is by division preferably by cutting through and removing rooted portions from the outer edges of established clumps seed propagation, in spring, should produce flowering plants after 4 or 5 years.

Common Gorse

The flowers can be seen all the year round, which led to the saying, that when the gorse is not in flower then kissing is out of fashion! In Scotland the bark has been used to produce a yellow dye, a very spiny evergreen shrub.

Growing Tips:

The fruit pod explodes when ripe, flinging the seeds some distance from the plant.

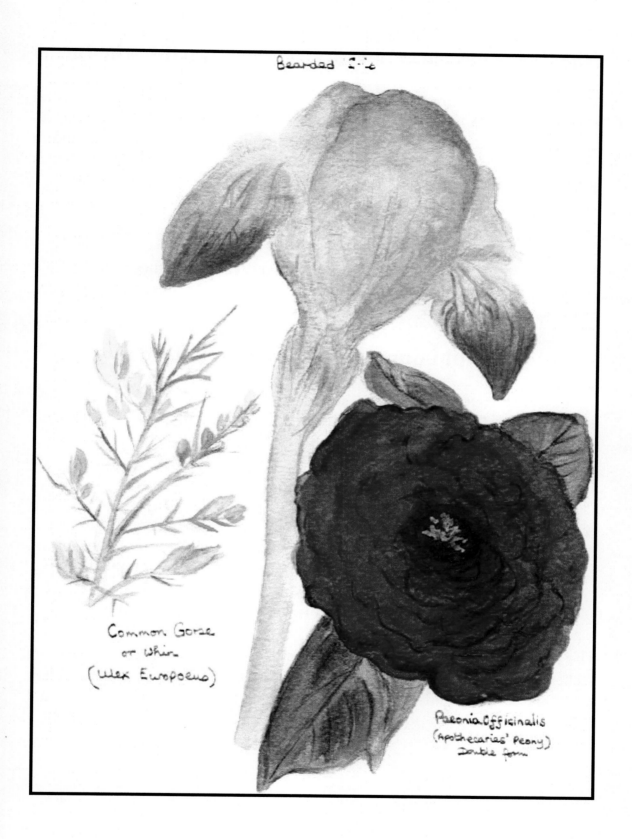

Bearded Iris

Common Gorse
or Whin
(Ulex Europoeus)

Paeonia Officinalis
(Apothecaries' Peony)
Double form

65

Nigella Damascena (Love-in-the-mist, Devil-in-the-bush)

The blue or white flowers of this beautiful 2ft. tall hardy annual, blooms all summer long in a haze of feathery, soft green foliage – love-in-the-mist. As the flowers fade, each seedpod of the bushy plant swells and ripens into a pale brown, red-barred, spiky globe – the-devil-in-the-bush. 'Miss Jekyll Blue' with semi-double blue flowers, is one of the finest of the cultivars.

Growing Tips:

Sow in the flowering site during spring, in successive batches (and, in mild areas, during autumn for early flowering.) Dead head unless you want seed heads, which can be dried for winter decoration, or self-sown seedlings.

Delphinium Large-flowered hybrids

Theatrical in stature, colour and sheer wealth of flowers on the stalk; they are the stars of the herbaceous border in June and July. The hybrids have large, flat flowers, often with a contrastingly coloured eye.

Growing Tips:

All delphiniums are fairly short lived and should be replaced every third year by young plants raised from basal cuttings or by division in spring. Discourage slugs with pellets, or sand around base.

Philadelphus 'Beauclerk' (Mock orange)

The common name for the genus Philadelphus is Mock orange, because the scent of its flowers is like that of orange blossom. The flowers of Beauclerk are single, broad petalled and about 2-2½" across. They appear in June and July.

Growing Tips:

Plant between autumn and spring, in any type of well-drained soil, in sun, or light shade. Propagate by cuttings under glass in summer, or in the open in autumn. Prune immediately after flowering by thinning out the older, twiggy-flowered whippy growths at the base.

Papaver orientale (Oriental Poppy)

Truly magnificent! In early June the buds split to reveal crumpled petals that uncurl into great bowls of brilliant Vermillion. The flowers rise to a height of 2-3ft. above spreading clumps of bristly foliage.

Growing Tips:

Plant in autumn 1½ to 2ft. apart. Propagate by root cuttings in late winter.

Jasminum Officinale (Common White Jasmine)

This Jasmine has been sweetening the evening air in British gardens since the 16th century. A vigorous, twining climber with a beauty to match its fragrance. Its clusters of small, white, primrose-like flowers are borne from June to October. In his essay on the 'Picturesque,' written in 1794, Sir Uvedale Price proposed that every cottage should have a porch so that Jasmine could wreath the door, I couldn't agree more!

Growing Tips:

Plant between autumn and spring, in any fertile well-drained soil in sun or shade, and then propagate in late summer by cuttings or layering and prune after flowering.

Love -in -a - Mist
(Nigella)
" Miss Jekyll
Blue "

Philadelphus (Mock orange)

Delphinium
Large flowered
hybrid

Papaver orientale
(oriental poppy)

Jasminum
Officinale

Portraits of Wild Flowers

The Buttercup Spell

Do you like butter? I'll easily tell,

for here I've a glittering spell!

Put your chin in the air, and below I'll hold,

My buttercup, polished and powdered with gold.

Ah – you love butter, that's easy to see,

For under your chin, as bright as can be,

Is a buttery shadow, golden and sweet,

that tells of the butter you're going to eat!

Portraits of Wild Flowers

I dedicate this page to my cousin Hazell, she loves fairies and elves

Midsummers Eve June 23rd is supposed
to be the most magical night of the year,
when you can see fairies, elves and other spirits.

The night is hot
and still not dark

Moths make circles
intent on the light

Tonight we're told
The shy fairies show themselves

The elves will dance
Round the magic ring

What a wonderful thing!
Whether you believe in them or not.

Lady's Smock

Shepherd's Purse

Bachelor's buttons

The Flowers

All the names I know from nurse:
Gardener's garters, Shepherd's purse,
Bachelor's buttons, Lady's smock,
And the lady Hollyhock.

Fairy places, fairy things,
Fairy woods where the wild bee wings,
Tiny trees for tiny dames —
These must all be fairy names!

Tiny woods below whose boughs
Shady fairies weave a house,
Tiny tree-tops, rose or thyme,
Where the braver fairies climb!

Fair are grown-up people's trees,
But the fairest woods are these;
Where, if I were not so tall,
I should live for good and all.

72

Rambler name unknown
(Dads Coopers Clase rose)

Dorothy Perkins

The Summer Sun

Oh, the sun shines bright in the Summer
And the breeze is soft as a sigh

Oh, the days are long in the Summer
And the Sun is King of the sky

Our Budgerigars – Parakeets small parrots

The aviary – home for our budgerigars, cockatiels and canaries. We have 35 budgerigars to date, many with beautiful colours. The budgerigars reproduce readily, and many are named. It is most interesting watching the babies being fed and fascinating to watch them practice flying or jumping up and down. The flight is an added attraction to the back garden as it is large enough to allow the birds to fly short distances. Some of our birds talk; "pretty boy" can be heard most days. A budgerigar spends many hours a day preening itself and partner; with great skill the long tail and wing feathers are pulled through the bill to remove every bit of dust or dirt. The small feathers are carefully pecked and smoothed, feet and toes too, are worked over with the bill. Every so often the head is rubbed over the oil gland above the base of the tail to grease the head feathers, and some fat is picked up in the bill, which is then evenly spread over the rest of the plumage. The thin oily layer on the feathers makes them water-repellant and prevents the bird from getting drenched in the rain and thus unable to fly.

Budgerigars in the flight

Babies have large eyes and streaks
covering the head

George and Georgina Cockatiels

Cockatiels 13" 32 cm

These kinds are amongst the most popular of parakeets, being ideal mixers and completely inoffensive to smaller companions. They are quiet birds and have become very tame. The cockatiel is perfectly hardy outside and if undisturbed a pair will breed, if provided with a large nest box. The hen has a yellow tail.

Georgina was found in our garden, she was eating rabbit food, which had spilt from the cage. I coaxed her into an old birds cage, she had a good feed of bird food and slept for hours, she could have come miles. I asked around if anyone was missing a cockatiel, but as nobody claimed her, we kept her; almost one year later and much to our surprise we were given a male cockatiel who was found in a friend's neighbours garden a couple of miles away. George met Georgina and they were compatible. We introduced them to the aviary and provided a large nest box. Georgina laid three eggs, but they never came to anything. It is so lovely to think that both cockatiels were lost and found a year apart and happily found each other.

Jason-Roller Canary

The Roller Canary is one of the few recent breeds of canary bred solely for its song. Jason sings so beautifully, he is a breathe of fresh air. Come rain or shine we can always rely on Jason to brighten our day.

Canaries have been in great demand as cage birds for over 300 years and along with the budgerigar are the most popular birds to be kept as pets.

Inside the Aviary

George

Georgina

Jason

Caterpillars are big eaters.

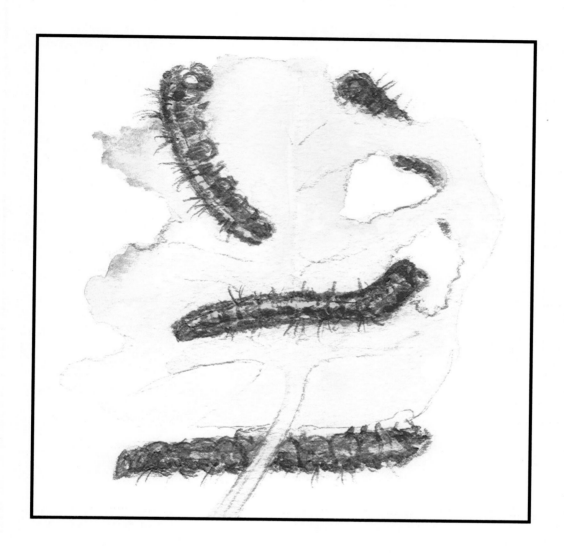

Is a caterpillar ticklish?

Well, it's always my belief

That he giggles, as he wriggles

Across a hairy leaf.

July — August

White Water Lily (Nymphaea alba)
Ponds and still waters may be covered with the round leaves of the
white water lily, which appear to support the flower. It blooms
from June to September. In Elizabethan times, those who wished to maintain
their chastity would eat the seeds and dry powdered stem!.

Gladiolus nanus
This dwarf comes in
many lovely colours and grows
in dainty sprays
My Mum's birthday flower

July
Dog Days bright and clear
Indicate a happy year.

August
If Bartlemy's Day be fair and clear
Then hope for a prosperous autumn that year.

A Bumble Bee

What do I see
A bumble bee
Sit on a rose
And wink at me!

What do you mean.
By hum, hum, hum
If you mean me
I dare not come

Deborah in Hebrew
means 'bee'

Hypericum 'Hidcote' (St John's wort)
The most spectacular
of late summer flowering. Rose of
shrubs, very easy to grow. Sharon
Dad gave me this bushy shrub
from a cutting, flowers up to 2in across.

Osteospermum
Star of the Veldt
(Rain Daisy)
'Glistening White'
From the South African country-
side comes this classic, silky
pure white flowering plant.
for the front of border in full sun.
Introduced to me by Mr King-
Invaluable.

Marigold
Calendula
officinalis
(Terry's birthday flower)
A very popular
garden plant which is
very hardy, and which will
give wonderful results from
a packet of seeds.

Garden Ornament
look·a·likes

Rebecca

These three beautiful ornaments really do
look just like Ruth, Rebecca and Matthew.
They were made at The Forge (Nurseries) by
Peter Fuller, a dear friend, several years
ago.

Matthew

Ruth

Buddleia Fallowiana 'Lochinch' "Butterfly Bush"

Less common (and less hardy) deciduous B Fallowiana maintains a weeping habit, about 6ft. high, and rather less across, with handsome woolly grey foliage. It flowers from July to September, deliciously scented 'Lochinch' hybrid is a clear soft lavender, each tiny flower having a tangerine eye.

Growing tips:

Plant in autumn or spring, in rich, well drained soil. In a sheltered side is best, in full sun. Propagate by heel cuttings only. Prune in March to maintain height and shape.

Hydrangea lacecap "Blue Wave"

The wild Hydrangea Macrophylla (syns H. Hortensis, H. Opuloides) comes from Japan. In its original state the blossom clusters are formed of two distinct components. In the centre of each flattened cluster are tiny fertile florets, and around the outside are others that are sterile and much longer. The overall effect is somewhat lacy, and cultivars have acquired the group name of Lacecap. "Blue Wave" is blue on acid soil and pink on alkaline soil. The plants thrive in the moist atmosphere and relative freedom from hard frost of that area, making rounded 5ft. high bushes, and very pretty, always excels itself.

Growing tips:

Plant in spring in humus rich, moist soil, shelter and dappled shape provides ideal conditions. Propagate by cuttings in a cold frame or greenhouse during summer. It flowers on wood of the previous year. Prune to shape after flowering.

Lavatera Olbia (Mallow)

My dear friend Pearl Mizen, gave me this bush. Mallows as Lavatera species are commonly called, have a rather old-fashioned cottage garden appearance. Although Lavatera Olbia has been growing in Britain for 400 years, it is today greatly under-used. It forms a 6-8ft. high bush of pithy stems that from late May-November put out pink flowers, beautiful and so reliable.

Growing tips:

Plant in early autumn or spring, in any ordinary, well-drained soil. The shrub needs full sun and shelter from cold winds. Propagate by cuttings and prune shoots by half, to avoid wind damage, in autumn, and cut hard back in spring to maintain shape.

Fuchsia Hybrid "Mrs. Popple"

A very elegant flower, that consists of a narrow tube that opens out into four petal-like sepals, below which is a bell of overlapping petals.

Growing tips:

Plant bedding Fuchsias in early summer, they need good, fertile soil, with full sun or light shade with some shelter. Before autumn lift and pot the plants and store them where they will be safe from frosts. Start into growth in spring and then propagate from cuttings for new bedding plants.

Campanula Garganica

Campanula Garganica, is outstanding among the larger, vigorous but not too rampant Campanulas.

Growing tips:

Plant in spring or autumn and propagate by division.

Lychnis Chalcedonica (Maltese Cross, Campion)

It forms sturdy clumps 3 to 4ft. tall stems. Each petal tip is boldly notched and although there are five instead of four, the overall effect is that of a Jerusalem or Maltese Cross.

Growing tips:

Plant from autumn to spring in ordinary fertile garden soil.

Crocosmia (Montbretia)

This popular bulbous plant was raised over 100 years ago as a cross between two less striking South African species- Crocosmia Aurea and C. Pottsil, it is vigorous.

Growing tips:

Plant in early spring 2" deep, 4" apart and propagate from cormlets in spring or from seeds.

Buddleia fallowiana
'Lochinch'

Red Admiral
Butterfly

Fuchsia hybrid
'Mrs Popple'

Lavatera
Olbia (Mallow)

Hydrangea Lacecap
'Blue Wave'

Campanula
garganica
(Bellflower)

Lychnis
chalcedonica
(Maltese Cross
Campion)

Crocosmia
(montbretia)

86

The Romantic Garden
Secret language that only flowers can reveal…

Flowers have and always will mean more than their beauty and perfume. The Victorians arranged their romantic meetings by using the language of flowers. Those who mastered floral communication could arrange 'secret lovers' meetings with floral clocks because certain flowers symbolised different times of the day.

Floral clocks altered four times a year because of the changing seasons. In a spring flora clock, the herb rosemary symbolised one o' clock, marjoram two, violet three, jonquil four, sweet pea five, broom six, tulip seven, bluebell eight, primrose nine, hawthorn ten, elderflower eleven, and carnation twelve.

Some conversations must have been hard going. Mr. X meets someone who takes his fancy. The next time he sees her he wears a daffodil buttonhole to show her his regard. At their next meeting, the lady who holds his affection just happens to be arranging flowers and is holding a Canterbury Bell, representing "acknowledgement."

Mr. X encouraged by this gesture, indicates his further intentions by arriving with a bunch of tiger lilies signalling passion – "my love has no bounds."

Much of the flower language originates in the Latin or Greek name for each plant. But some names and meanings were given because the flowers resemble some other object. Aster, with its fanciful resemblance to a star, comes from the Latin aster for star. In flower language it means "afterthought." Shakespeare, Chaucer and great poets included the language of flowers in their works, and so too have hymns.

Telephones, motorways and high technology may have shifted communication to a different level but the hidden words can still be voiced in the fragrance and petals of a humble flower and our gardens may even be talking to us:

Daisy · innocence, Bindweed · persistence, cannot accept your answer, Ivy · I am attached to you, Lavender · silence, Hawthorn hope, Speedwell · fidelity, Dandelion · oracle, Lilac · love stirs in me, Hyacinth · fun, Forget-me-not · remembrance and faith.

Feverfew

Marjoram

Mint

Thyme

Sage

Spring-Summer flowering
Pansy - Hybrid
see page 6

The PANSY
means "thinking
of you".

The herbs on this page
are grown through the
sections of a cartwheel
which lies flat raised
off the soil by a layer of
bricks, practical and decorative.
Added attraction to the herb

Rosemary   Kitchen Garden. Chives

Comfrey

Lavender

89

Eschscholzia Californica (Californian Poppy)

The California poppy glorifies the garden with a bright flower display that lasts from June to October, and complements it, too, with its exquisitely cut, blue-green foliage. 'Orange King' is 15" tall, the crumpled silk petals fall to reveal long, cylindrical seed pods.

Growing tips:

Sow outdoors in spring, or in autumn under cloches, thin seedlings to 6" apart. The plants thrive in sandy, poor soil and in full sun, seeding themselves freely.

Dianthus – Pinks

These superb plants are ideal for the front of a border or bed, about 10-15" tall, have grassy, grey-green leaves and bear a profusion of flowers from early summer to early autumn, and they are richly scented, bursting with petals and come in a range of bright colours.

Growing tips:

Plant in autumn or spring, 10-12" apart, setting them shallowly in limy to neutral soil with sharp drainage, Avoid mulches and remove dead leaves round the stems where moisture might collect. Position the plants in full sun, and water them only in excessively dry spells. Easily increased from cuttings from non-flowering sideshoots in late summer, root in sand.

Painted Lady · Butterfly – Vanessa Cardui

Eschscholzia californica
Californian Poppy

Dianthus
Pinks

Painted Lady

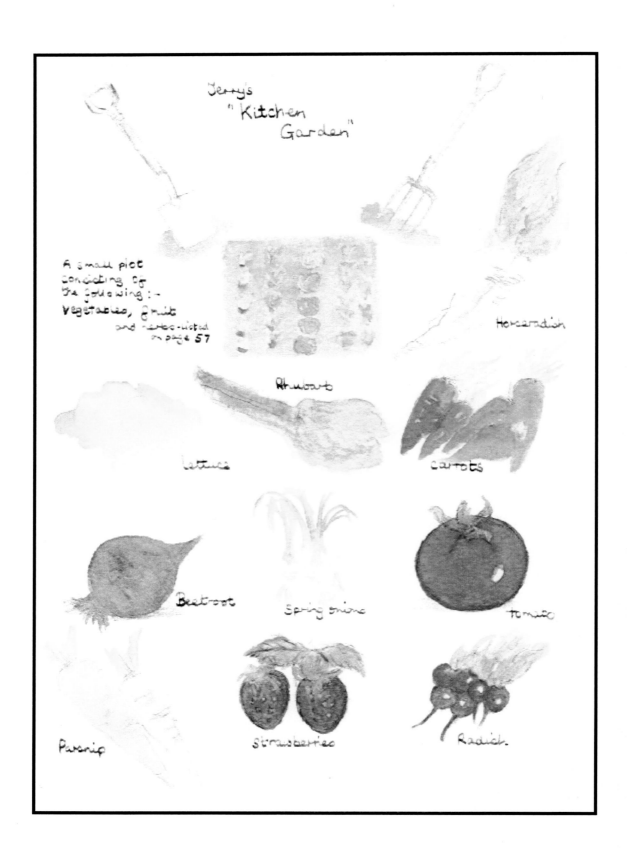

Jerry's "Kitchen Garden"

A small plot consisting of the following :-
Vegetables, fruit and herbs-listed on page 57

Horseradish

Rhubarb

Lettuce

Carrots

Beetroot

Spring onions

Tomato

Parsnip

Strawberries

Radish.

Garden Visitors

All things bright and beautiful
All creatures great and small,
All things wise and wonderful,
The Lord God made them all.

Each little flower that opens,
Each little bird that sings,
He made their glowing colours,
He made their tiny wings!

The surface of the ground is alive with small
creatures such as centipedes, ground beetles and
the earth worm, an invertebrate whose contribution
is essential to the fertility of the earth as it breaks down nutrients
and aerates the soil.

Acanthus Spinosus (Bear Breeches)

The Romans and Greeks wove Acanthus into garlands and draped them about their houses, their furniture and themselves; and they immortalised their fondness for the plant by carving Acanthus foliage upon the capitals of the Corinthian Columns that supported so many of the public buildings. The leaves of Acanthus Spinosus are large and often at least 2ft. long, dark green, hairy and deeply cut. The splendid flower spikes, 4-5ft. tall, are crowded with mauve and white hooded flowers in late summer. Both the tips of the leaves and the calyces (outer protective parts) of the flowers are spiny, and can scratch the unwary. Even so this species is usually preferred to others less spiky, because of its splendid flowers.

Growing tips:

Plant between autumn and spring, in fertile, well-drained soil. Then propagate in winter by root cuttings or in spring by seeds (can spread exuberantly.)

Scabiosa Purple Scabious

Worth growing for cut flowers alone, this is also a fine plant for backing pinks (Dianthus) in the border. Together they provide a softly coloured display all summer through.

Growing tips:

Plant in spring, 18" apart, in ordinary garden soil, preferably limy, and in full sun. Dead- head regularly. Propagate by division in spring.

Gaillardia

Blanket flowers make excellent cut flowers. Daisy like blooms, 2ft. tall.

Growing tips:

Plant in spring 12" apart in well drained soil and propagate by division or root cuttings.

Chrysanthemum Maximum (Shasta Daisy)

The Shasta Daisy, came to Britain from the Pyrenees in the early 19th century. It is about 3ft. tall. Its bold white, yellow-eyed blooms will make a splendid show anywhere.

Growing tips:

Plant in spring 15" apart in well-drained soil. Propagate by cuttings or by division of established clumps.

Solidago (Golden Rod)

Solidago 'Crown of Rays' adds a vivid patch of yellow to the garden.

Growing tips:

Plant from autumn to spring, 2ft, apart and propagate by division, it will self-seed.

Alchemilla Mollis (Lady's Mantle)

Lady's Mantle was alleged to have played a part in alchemy, the art of turning base metal into gold; hence it's botanical name. It is a beautiful plant that forms a 12" high clump of pleated, downy, grey-green leaves, in which dewdrops are caught and gleam in the early morning sun like beads of mercury. Above the foliage, dense sprays of tiny, cool green-yellow flowers are produced from early June to August.

Growing tips:

Plant in autumn or spring (it self sows freely) Thanks to Mr. Thompson, a dear friend, I now have lots of plants from the plant he gave me.

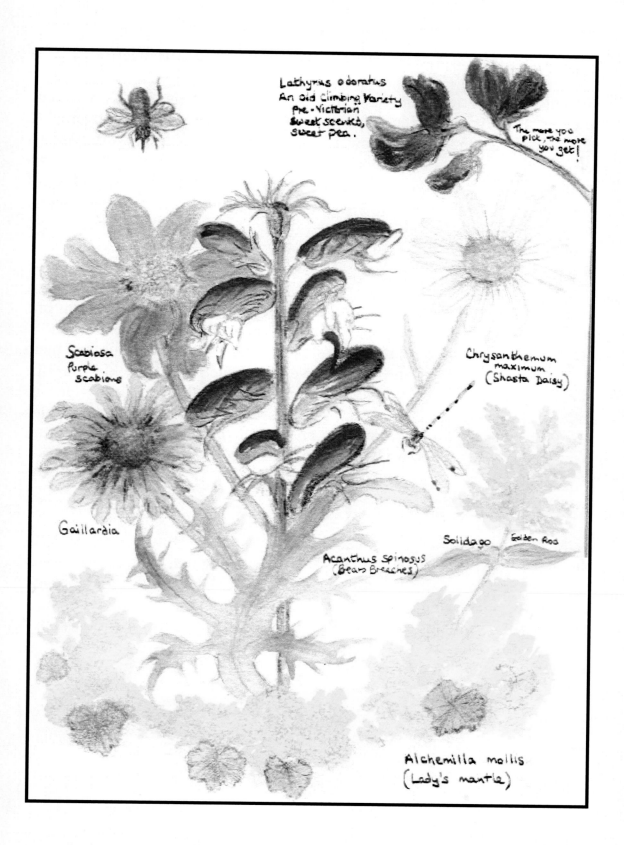

Lathyrus odoratus
An Old Climbing Variety
Pre-Victorian
sweet scented,
sweet pea.

The more you pick, the more you get!

Scabiosa
Purple
Scabious

Chrysanthemum
maximum
(Shasta Daisy)

Gaillardia

Solidago   Golden Rod

Acanthus spinosus
(Bears Breaches)

Alchemilla mollis
(Lady's mantle)

Passiflora Caerulea (Common Passion Flower)

When Spanish Priests first saw this plant growing in the forests of Brazil, they regarded it as a token that the Indians would one day be converted to Christianity for there in the flowers were what they took to be the symbols of Christ's Passion. Each bloom opens flat to reveal an outer circle of ten white petals (the disciples, minus Judas and Peter); within these, a ring of fine purple-blue filaments (the crown of thorns); and in the centre, conspicuous anthers and stigmas (the nails); while the wounds are represented by five yellowish stains.

The flowers are 3" across, and in good years they are followed by orange, egg-shaped fruits. The plant climbs rapidly by its tendrils to 20-30ft. and has evergreen leaves like open hands, flowers continuous from June – September. My dad grew these Passiflora's from seeds, I encouraged them to climb up the trellis and tumble over the Dutch Honeysuckle over the porch, and they appear to be good companions, both are a little vigorous and need a good prune in spring. The Passion fruit of Passiflora Caerulea are green turning to soft apricot-orange, and they seldom ripen and are barely edible if they do, we have had a magnificent show of fruit.

Growing tips:

Mild gardens are suitable, plant during late spring in any type of well-drained soil, in sun or light shade, against a sheltered wall with trellis or wire supports. Propagate in summer by stem cuttings under glass. Prune hard in spring, cutting out dead stems at ground level and shortening side-shoots to 6" from their base. My Dad grew three from seed, which I planted together, thinking we may lose one or two if hit by frost, but all three survived. Such a magnificent show of flowers and fruit.

Passiflora Caerulea
(Common Passion flower)

Fruits of
Passiflora
Caerulea

Monarda Didyma 'Cambridge Scarlet' (Sweet Bergamot)

This is one of the finest herbs for the border, exciting in colour and form and highly aromatic. The flowers are rich in nectar, so they are usually buzzing with bees, and the leaves can be dried and infused to make a herbal tea. The most brilliant variety is 'Cambridge Scarlet' whose 3ft. tall stalks, bearing bright green oval, hairy leaves all the way up, are crowned with large clusters of small, tabular, bright scarlet flowers from June – September. As each cluster develops, another inch or two of stem grows from the middle of it, topped with a second, smaller whorl.

Growing tips:

Plant between autumn and spring 15-18" apart in fertile, moist soil and in full sun or light shade. Cut stems down in late winter and divide in the dormant season.

Penstemon Campanulatus

The vivid foxglove – like flowers and evergreens, foliage of Penstemon look splendid in the mixed border, reaching 1-2ft. high. A fine flush of blooms appear in mid June and if flowers are removed as soon as they have faded the display will continue until the end of September.

Growing tips:

Plant in spring 12" apart, in ordinary garden soil, in full sun or partial shade, and propagate by seeds.

Eccremocarpus Scaber (Chilean Glory Flower)

After planting rapidly climbs to a height of 10ft. Self seeds.

Clematis Jackmanii Superba

This is the best known and most popular of all hybrid Clematis and justly so. The velvety, dark purple, white centred flowers are enormous – up to 6" across, and plentiful. If the plant is pruned almost to the ground in early spring it will climb up to 10-12 feet by midsummer. It is on the new growth that the flowers appear, most abundantly in July but continuing into October if it does not become too dry. My Dad gave me this Clematis.

Growing tips:

Plant between autumn and late spring and they will thrive in neutral to alkaline soil of average fertility and with good drainage; it resents root disturbance.

Althaea Rosea (Hollyhock)

Hollyhock's have been favourite garden flowers for centuries. A hundred years ago, until the outbreak of rust disease, they were cultivated as perennials by specialist growers, and on hundreds of named varieties. The disease is kept at bay nowadays by treating Hollyhocks either as annuals or as biennials. They flower from July and continue well into autumn.

Growing tips:

As an annual, sow seeds under glass in early spring; prick off singly into 4" pots and plant outside in late spring.

Lonicera Japonica 'Halliana'

Splendidly vigorous, the climate is not warm and moist enough for it to outgrow its welcome, it flowers June – October and often until Christmas. The young stems are decorated with small clusters of tubular scented flowers, opening white and turning yellow as they age. 'Halliana' has an unforgettable fragrance.

Growing tips:

Plant in spring, in well-drained soil, in full sun or light shade. Propagate by cuttings in summer or autumn by layering or by seeds.

The Fairy Miniature Rose

It flowers in June and July, and usually put on a second performance in autumn.

Growing tips:

Plant in October/November, or in March, in any good, well-drained soil and propagate by budding in summer or by hardwood cuttings in autumn.

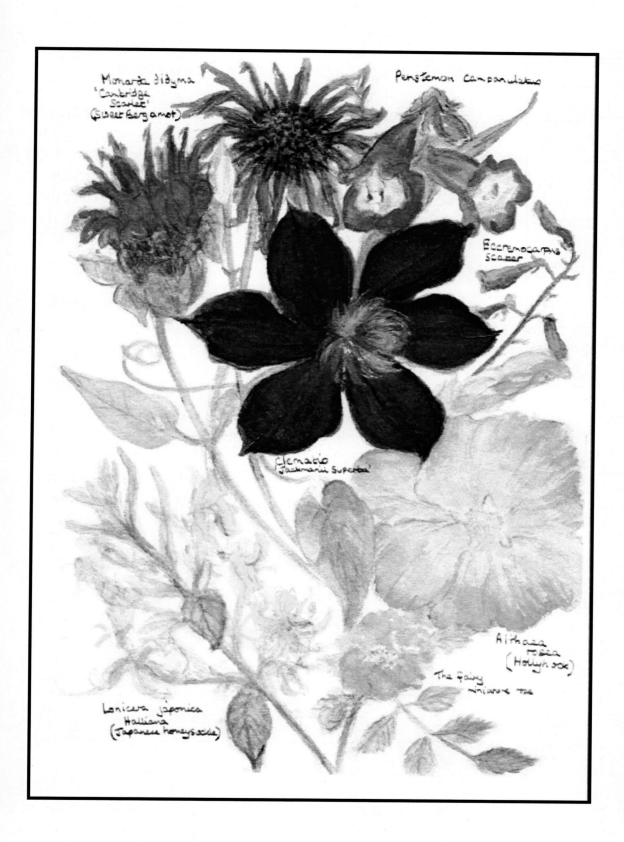

Monarda didyma
'Cambridge
Scarlet'
(Sweet Bergamot)

Penstemon campanulatus

Eccremocarpus
Scaber

Clematis
'Jackmanii Superba'

Althaea
rosea
(Hollyhock)

The Fairy
miniature rose

Lonicera japonica
Halliana
(Japanese honeysuckle)

Lysimachia Punctata (Yellow Loosestrife)

The yellow loosestrife, a native of Asia Minor, has escaped from gardens to grow wild in several places in Britain. It makes great clumps of growth, and is especially vigorous by the waterside or in a bog garden. From June to August the 3 foot high stems carry spikes of cup-shaped, bright yellow flowers that look like those of the Allied Lysimachia Nummulana (creeping jenny.)

Growing tips:

Plant between autumn and spring, 1½-2 foot apart, in any soil, even heavy clay, that is permanently moist. Cut stems down in autumn and can be divided in the dormant season.

Hemerocallis Flava (Day Lily)

The flowers of Day Lilies – as the genus Hemerocallis is popularly known – each last for only one day. But the shortness of their life is compensated for by the freshness of each new daily crop. Hemerocallis Flava is a robust, spreading Day Lily, richly scented blooms on bare stems from late May – to early July.

Growing tips:

Plant between autumn and spring, 18" apart, more for large-growing cultivars, less for miniatures. All thrive in ordinary garden soil. Leave established clumps undisturbed until they become overcrowded and then divide during dormancy.

Anemone Hybrida

The rose-pink anemone was given to me by Brian Sykes my neighbour. The white and deep rose flowers of this group of anemone hybrids are the result of crossing two oriental anemones, the Japanese Anemone (Hupehensis Japonica) and the Nepalese A Vitifolium, and it is from this second parent that the hybrids derive their handsome, dark green, vine-like leaves. The oldest named selections – fine 4-5ft. high plants that carry a succession of wide, saucer-shaped flowers from August to October. Include the lovely white flowered 'Honorine Jobert' and the rose-pink 'Mont Rose.'

Growing tips:

Plant between October and March in ant fertile, well-drained but moisture-retentive soil, ideally in partial shade. Cut to ground level after flowering and propagate by division between October and March, but leave newly planted specimens undisturbed for the first few years.

Campanula Persicifolia (Peach-Leaved Bellflower)

This old-fashioned cottage-garden plant has been with us since the 16th century at least. It forms wide clumps of interlocking rosettes of narrow, leathery, evergreen leaves from which flowering stems push up to a slender 3-4 feet. Between June and August, these are hung with cup shaped, nodding blooms. Cut down faded spikes to encourage fresh flowers.

Growing tips:

Plant in early autumn or late spring, in any good, well-drained soil, in full sun or light shade and space 18" apart; and dead-head after flowering. Propagate by division in autumn or spring.

Malva Moschata (Musk Mallow)

Not only is the Musk Mallow one of our most beautiful wild flowers, it is a champion in the border too. It forms a 3ft. high bush of finely cut, light green foliage, above which silky open flowers of pure white nod all summer through.

Growing tips:

Plant in autumn or spring, 12-15" apart in ordinary well-drained soil, and propagate by basal cuttings or by seeds in spring.

Hemerocallis
Day Lily

Anemone
hybrida
"Mont Rose"

"Honorine Jobert"

Lysimachia
Punctata
Yellow loosestrife

Campanula
Persicifolia
'Snowdrift'

Campanula Persicifolia
Telhah
Beauty

Malva
Moschata
Musk Mallow

A Dragonfly

When the heart of the summer made drowsy the land
A dragonfly came and sat on my hand
With its blue jointed body and wings like spunglass
It lit on my fingers as though they were glass

Autumn Song

These are the days of falling leaves
The days of hazy weather,
Smelling of gold chrysanthemums
And grey wood smoke together

These are the nights of nearby stars
The nights of clear moons,
When the windy darkness echoes
To crickets farewell tunes.

Heather
or Ling
(Calluna
Vulgaris)

Hebe
'Autumn Glory'
Shrubby Veronica

Height 2ft
Spread 2ft

(Invaluable, Dad gave this hebe to me)
Best Aug-Sept

One of the hardiest and latest-
flowering of the hebes, 'Autumn
Glory' carries its intense violet
spikes almost until the first frosts.
It thrives in mild coastal
areas, even in windswept
places where few other
shrubs will survive.
The dark evergreen foliage
makes it a valued year round
resident of the mixed or
shrub border, needs slightly
each year.

Growing tips
Plant in autumn or spring or
from container at any time of
the year in well-drained
fertile soil in full sun
Propagate by semi-hardwood
cuttings during autumn.

110

September — October

Callistephus chinensis (China aster)
The bright yellow centres of these
daisy-like, single-flowered china asters
show off the strong purple of the petals.
                                    (My Dad's birthday flower)
Growing tips.
Sow directly in the flowering site. Sunny wind sheltered.
Make occasional sowings at regular intervals
to extend the flowering season.

September
St Matthew
Brings on cold dew.

October.
Much rain in October
Much wind in December

Dandelion Taraxacum officinalis
These flowers grow in Britain but only
in wild grassland areas
The plant is difficult to control as it
has long tap roots, which can produce
new plants if they are cut or broken.
The common dandelion is very useful,
for its young leaves, make a tasty
salad when blanched, and the cooked green
leaves are a substitute for spinach.
The roots are used in some countries as a
coffee substitute, and the flowers make a
good wine.

Meconopsis Cambrica
Welsh Poppy

I love these beautiful bright yellow Welsh Poppies,
they really brighten up my the garden, they love damp, rock places, 12"
high,
They flower continuous throughout the summer.
I prefer them in clumps. My dear friend and neighbour David Threader
gave me the poppy seeds, as I've always admired the Welsh Poppies in his
garden.

Growing tips:

Plant in spring 12" apart, in ordinary garden soil, moist or dry, and in sun
or shade. Cut back to ground level in autumn. Propagate by seeds sown or
when ripe.

The Red Admiral

The butterflies arrive in Britain from the continent in May and breed here
during the summer and autumn. No garden should be without beautiful
butterflies.

Red Admiral   Welsh Poppy
MECONOPSIS CAMBRICA

Harvest

My favourite hymn:-
We plough the fields and scatter
The good seed on the land,
But it is fed, and watered
By God's almighty hand.
He sends the snow in winter,
The warmth to swell the grain,
The breezes and the sunshine,
And soft refreshing rain.

All good gifts around us
Are sent from heaven above,
Then thank the lord, O thank the Lord,
For all his love.

We thank thee then, O Father,
For all things bright and good,
The seed-time and the harvest,
Our life, our health, our food,
No gifts have we to offer
For all thy love imparts,
But that which thou desirest,
Our humble, thankful hearts.

November — December

November
No warmth, no cheerfulness, no healthful ease,
No comfortable feel in any member,
No shade, no shine, no butterflies, no bees,
No fruits, no flowers, no leaves
No birds – No-vember

December
Frost on the shortest day
bodes a bad winter

Chrysanthemum (Jerry's Mum's birthday flower)
    coccineum
3ft tall, with bright green, ferny leaves
and flowers that range from white through
pinks to reds
An admirable border perennial for early Summer

Growing tips – Plant 15in apart, in spring, well drained, but moisture-
retentive soil is essential. Propagate by cuttings of basal
                                        shoots in Spring.

Ilex
(Common Holly)
Holly is one of the most popular of
evergreens. Even without regular
clipping, they are of fairly compact
habit and grow reasonably slowly,
eventually reaching a height
of 10-30ft. The female forms
are the most colourful, for it is
these that bear the berries.
    In most cases, male hollies
    are required to pollinate the
females, and should be planted
within a few yards from them.

Growing tips –
Plant all hollies as young pot-
grown specimens in autumn or
spring. Any well drained soil will do
Propagate in late summer or autumn
by cuttings in a cold frame.

115

Himalayan Honeysuckle

Leycesteria Caprifoliaceae

The only species grown widely in nineteenth-
century gardens was the plant most frequently
seen to-day, Leycesteria formosa, a fairly
hardy, deciduous Himalayan plant with purplish bell-
like flowers, introduced in 1824. Absolutely lovely this yr!
In Britain the fruits are greatly appreciated by pheasants
and it is sometimes planted as game cover.

Growing tips – Plant between autumn and spring, in
ordinary, well drained soil, sun or light shade.
Propagate by seeds in spring, or by root cuttings
outdoors in Autumn.

Remembrance Day.

to Some
The Poppy is the somme
And blood, dead sons,
Remembrance and forgetting

to me
It is the fragile wavering hope
Of one day
All suns neversetting

Hurt no living thing

Hurt no living thing
Ladybird, nor butterfly
Nor moth with dusty wing
Nor cricket chirping cheerily
Nor grasshopper so light of leap
Nor dancing gnat or beetle fat
Nor harmless worms that creep.

The twelfth month is here. The trees are bare but the evergreens brighten our days.

'Our Dear Pets'

Bob

Victoria & Albert

Cottontail

Misty

Barney

Christmas Day

Nature's decorations glisten
For above their usual trim,
Birds on box and laurels listen
As so near the cherubs hymn.

Boreas now no longer winters
On the desolated coast,
Oaks no more are m'u'n in splinters
By the whirlwind and his host.

Spinks and Ouzles sing sublimely
'We too have a saviour born'
Whiter blossoms burst untimely
On the blest Mosaic thorn

God all bounteous, all creative
Whom no ills from good dissuade
Is incarnate, and a native
Of the very world he made.

And so the year draws to its close - but it isn't the end - just a new beginning

Full Circle

While writing this book we have turned the full circle of one calendar year and watched the four seasons come and go.

We have watched the flowers around us but their circles are closed, beginning and ending with the seed, continuous birth and death and rebirth.

Now the Jasmine is in full bloom again and the circle is complete. I hope you have enjoyed the flowers which have taken part in this book.

I have enjoyed my years labour both in the garden and in Ivy Studio (my little honey pot) which Terry built specially for me. It is now closed for the winter.

P. T. O

In Conclusion :-

The Answer

In the tiny petal
        Of a tiny flower
            that grew from a tiny pod...
To the miracle
        and the mystery
            Of all creation and God.

forget-me-not

This book is dedicated to my loving husband & family
whose loving support made it possible, it is also a loving
tribute to my dear Dad, who sadly died from lung cancer.
His love of life, his cheery whistle, like the blackbird in spring,
inspired me to love nature, record it and share it with you.